Cloud Software Development Life Cycle (Cloud SDLC)

Elmozamil Elamir

Cloud Software Development Life Cycle (Cloud SDLC)

Introduction & Foundation

LAP LAMBERT Academic Publishing

Impressum / Imprint

Bibliografische Information der Deutschen Nationalbibliothek: Die Deutsche Nationalbibliothek verzeichnet diese Publikation in der Deutschen Nationalbibliografie; detaillierte bibliografische Daten sind im Internet über http://dnb.d-nb.de abrufbar.

Alle in diesem Buch genannten Marken und Produktnamen unterliegen warenzeichen-, marken- oder patentrechtlichem Schutz bzw. sind Warenzeichen oder eingetragene Warenzeichen der jeweiligen Inhaber. Die Wiedergabe von Marken, Produktnamen, Gebrauchsnamen, Handelsnamen, Warenbezeichnungen u.s.w. in diesem Werk berechtigt auch ohne besondere Kennzeichnung nicht zu der Annahme, dass solche Namen im Sinne der Warenzeichen- und Markenschutzgesetzgebung als frei zu betrachten wären und daher von jedermann benutzt werden dürften.

Bibliographic information published by the Deutsche Nationalbibliothek: The Deutsche Nationalbibliothek lists this publication in the Deutsche Nationalbibliografie; detailed bibliographic data are available in the Internet at http://dnb.d-nb.de.

Any brand names and product names mentioned in this book are subject to trademark, brand or patent protection and are trademarks or registered trademarks of their respective holders. The use of brand names, product names, common names, trade names, product descriptions etc. even without a particular marking in this work is in no way to be construed to mean that such names may be regarded as unrestricted in respect of trademark and brand protection legislation and could thus be used by anyone.

Coverbild / Cover image: www.ingimage.com

Verlag / Publisher:
LAP LAMBERT Academic Publishing
ist ein Imprint der / is a trademark of
OmniScriptum GmbH & Co. KG
Heinrich-Böcking-Str. 6-8, 66121 Saarbrücken, Deutschland / Germany
Email: info@lap-publishing.com

Herstellung: siehe letzte Seite /
Printed at: see last page
ISBN: 978-3-659-77826-1

Table of Content

Title	Page

Chapter One

Introduction

Chapter Two

Cloud Computing

Chapter Three

Software as a Service

Chapter Four

Analysis of SDLC for Cloud Computing

Chapter Five

Recommended SDLC Characteristics

Chapter Six

Conclusion and Recommendation

List of Figures

Dedication

To my family,,,

To my friends,,,

To every researcher,,,

I dedicate my effort

Acknowledgement

Many thanks to everyone who contributed directly or indirectly with advise, valuable support and academic support. Many thanks to everybody who I asked or discussed something related to this research with him.

Abstract

Nowadays cloud computing and software engineering are the two of most interesting and hot topics.

Software engineering is a well-established field for the design and development of software systems that support each type of enterprise from the midsize to the large-scale. The software development life cycle (SDLC) consisting of requirements, design and development phases. There are also many frameworks and methodologies for such design, development and implementation of software systems. Depending on the application domain, there are proven function-oriented and object-oriented and component-based methodologies as well as service-oriented and agile frameworks.

Cloud computing provides many benefits for organizations to get the opportunity to invest in their works and focus on their area of specializations by providing state of art technology for infrastructure, software, database, etc... using different methods of payments.

Now cloud computing providers face many difficulties to support different culture, processes and procedures with software.

This book will try to provide the basic understanding of these limitations and ideas about how to think about the development.

Chapter One

Introduction

1.1 Introduction

Enterprises relay on the information technology to run their business to support and simplify the complexity of the business operations. Each successive technology 'revolution' promises tremendous gains.

Software engineering is a well-established field for the design and development of software systems that support each type of enterprise from the midsize to the large-scale. The software development life cycle (SDLC) consisting of requirements, design and development phases. There are also many frameworks and methodologies for such design, development and implementation of software systems. Depending on the application domain, there are proven function-oriented and object-oriented and component-based methodologies as well as service-oriented and agile frameworks.

With the emergence of cloud computing, however, there is a need for the traditional approaches to software construction to be adapted to take full advantage of the cloud technologies.

Cloud computing is an attractive paradigm for business organizations due to the enormous benefits it promises, including savings on capital expenditure and availability of cloud-based services on demand and in real time. Organizations can self-provision software development platforms, together with infrastructure if so required, to develop and deploy applications much more speedily. Since the cloud environment is dynamic, visualized, distributed and multi-tenant, necessary characteristics that cloud-enabled software must exhibit need to be

2

inherently built into the software systems. This is epically so if the software is to be deployed in the cloud environment or made available for access by multiple cloud consumers. In this context, it is imperative to recognize that cloud SDLC is an accelerated process and that software development needs to be more iterative and incremental. Also, the application architecture must provide characteristics to leverage cloud infrastructure capabilities such as storage connectivity and communications. It is important that the chosen frameworks are suitable for fast cycle deployments. Methodologies must also ensure satisfaction of consumer demands of performance, availability, security, privacy, reliability and, above all, scalability and multi-tenancy.

Cloud computing is a large-scale distributed computing paradigm that is driven by economies of scale, in which a pool of abstracted, virtualized, dynamically-scalable, managed computing power, storage, platforms, and services are delivered on demand to external customers over the Internet.

Publicly available cloud computing began with the launch of Amazon's Elastic Compute Cloud, offering Infrastructure as a Service. Soon afterwards, Google launched it Google App Engine, which took a different path, offering a development Platform as a Service. In due course, Microsoft took a path similar to Google's, with its recently launched Azure platform.

Could computing is an emerging paradigm that allows cloud consumers to self-provision cloud-based IT resources. As a result, enterprise are positioning their on-promise software applications (and hardware resources) to enable them to take advantage of the distributed nature of the cloud environment. Although, software engineering (SE) is a well-established engineering discipline with numerous software development approaches, unless the on-premise applications are aligned with distributed computing paradigm, the benefits that cloud computing promises cannot be fully realized. The cloud computing paradigm has, therefore, caused to change the conventional business models and application development approaches. In this context, the software engineers and enterprise architects are adopting new ways for the design, development, integration and deployment of the enterprise-wide applications, this is mainly due to the fact that conventional SE processes do not necessarily and satisfactorily lend to the development of software that is service-oriented and fit for distributed computing environment such as cloud computing. As a result, SE frameworks and methodologies suitable for migration of enterprise applications to cloud environments.

1.2 Problem Statements

Investigate SE frameworks that are suitable for software development to take advantage of the benefits that cloud computing offers and to fill a gap in the SE literature and practice by providing scientific contributions focusing on SE methods suitable for cloud computing environment.

1.3 Research Questions

1. What is the impact of Cloud Computing in the Software Development Life Cycle (SDLC)?
2. Will traditional SDLC frameworks be suitable completely for the cloud SDLC?
3. How is the traditional SDLC different from Cloud SDLC?
4. What is the software engineering best practice that is applicable in cloud computing software development?

4

1.4 Research objectives

1. Discuss and analyze the implications of cloud computing paradigm on SE methods and frameworks to develop best practices for the SE industry.
2. To capture the state-of-the-art research and practice with respect to SE for enterprise cloud environments.
3. To discuss and analyze the implications of cloud computing on SE methods, techniques and frameworks.
4. To identify potential research directions and technologies to facilitate software process improvement initiatives.
5. To explore limitations and barriers with respect to design and development of software suitable for cloud environments.
6. To discuss and establish best practices for software development industry with reference to Enterprise Cloud Computing.

1.5 Research Scope

Software development life cycle as well as software development life cycle frameworks/methodologies also a lot of new published papers, books, post and best practice are studied in order to understand and analyze SDLC and suggest/recommend methodologies that fit for cloud computing software development life cycle.

1.6 Research methodologies

The research will focus on understanding the existing software engineering methodologies and the cloud computing paradigm to analyze, and compare it with the environment to suggest which software engineering methodology/

methodologies are more applicable for cloud computing paradigm and the limitation in each one.

1.7 Research Organization

This research is organized in six chapters:

Chapter One: is research proposal, this chapter outlines the problem statement, research objectives, research methodologies, research key questions.

Chapter Two: this chapter is about cloud computing and paradigm shift that occur in computing environment, moving from traditional environment to distributed cloud computing environment.

Chapter Three: this chapter discusses the software as a service SaaS as it is the most important part of software cloud computing.

Chapter Four: this chapter discusses SDLC phases and analyzes the impact of cloud computing on each phase.

Chapter Five: Recommended SDLC characteristics

Chapter Six: Conclusion and Recommendation.

Chapter Two

Cloud Computing

2.1 Introduction

Each large enterprises has to continuously evaluate the state-of-art technology and architectures and plan their IT environment, and also 'keeping the lights on' by ensuring the system and business stability (Shroff G., 2010).

Many years ago many companies relies on their installed application on their desktops, any update, upgrade, and hotfixes should be installed in any desktop. In client server model the application is installed in the server maybe hosted in data center and installation done once in the server but we still need to install clients and apply updates, upgrades, and hotfixes in server for the application and on all desktops for client application.

Could computing describes the movement toward using wide area networks (WANs), Internet technology, distributed database system and software implementation technologies (Raines G., 2009).

Cloud computing service providers take the opportunity of the needs for software from midsized and small companies that need technology and the need to focus on their own work and removing the overhead of maintain software, storage, platform by their own, so the ask a service provider to provide the server (outsourcing) and focus on their own work.

Enterprise Computing

"Enterprise computing is the use of computers for data processing in large organizations, also referred to as information systems (IS), or even information technology (IT) in general" (Shorff G., 2010).

Datacenter is a collection of servers hosted in a room or prepared area that is will configured to host servers so users can subscribe and use applications installed in servers, the datacenter accessed through WAN and/or internet (Anthony T. Velte, Toby J. Velte, Robert Elsenpeter, 2010).

Virtualization

"Virtualization server is a software can be installed allowing multiple instances of virtual servers to be used. In this way, you can have a half a dozen virtual servers running on one physical server" (Anthony T. Velte, Toby J. Velte, Robert Elsenpeter, 2010).

Distributed server

Of course not all of the servers always hosted in the same datacenter it may be hosted oversees or at different location in same building, distributed server will provide the service as if it were hosted in the same location (Anthony T. Velte, Toby J. Velte, Robert Elsenpeter, 2010).

This implementation gives the service provider more flexibility in options, security, availability and reliability of the service. For example Google has their server installed all over the globe (Anthony T. Velte, Toby J. Velte, Robert Elsenpeter, 2010).

2.2 Cloud Computing

A large number of computers connected through a communication network like WAN or Internet, these computers distributed over a network and has ability to run applications on many connected computers at the same time.

"Cloud computing is a large-scale distributed computing paradigm that is driven by economies of scale, in which a pool of abstracted, virtualized, dynamically-scalable, managed computing power, storage, platforms, and services are delivered on demand to external customers over the internet" (I. Foster, Y. Zhau, R. Loan, S. Lu, 2008).

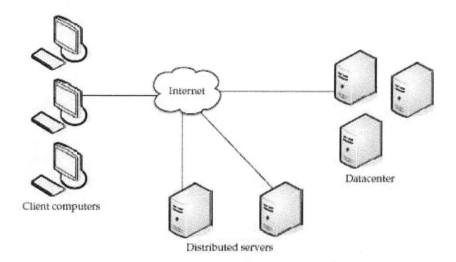

Fig 2.1: Cloud Computing Solution (Anthony T. Velte, Toby J. Velte, Robert Elsenpeter, 2010).

The need for standard definition is always what we want to understand the concept.

As defined by The National Institute of Standard and Technology (NIST), Information Technology Laboratory *"Cloud computing is a pay-per-use model for enabling available, convenient, on-demand network access to a shared pool of configurable computing resources (e.g., networks, servers, storage, applications, services) that can be rapidly provisioned and released with minimal management effort or service provider interaction"* (David S. Linticum, 2009)

Could computing is available publicly by hosting uploading files SkyeDrive, or public personal data Facebook, photos Instgram, watching and sharing videos Youtube and many others. It began with the launch of Amazon's Elastic Compute Cloud, offering Infrastructure as a Service, and also Google launched its Google App Engine which offering a development Platform as a Service, also Microsoft provide Azure platform (ShrofG.f, 2010).

2.2.1 Cloud Computing Enablers

The continuous evolution of information technology enable the applicability of cloud computing nowadays one terabit disk is installed in any computer, high speed connectivity and software evolution. Below are some of these enablers (Eric A. Marks, Bob Lozano, 2010):

- Commodity Hardware.
- Network Speed.
- Virtualization.

- Application Architectures.
- Data Storage Architectures.
- Pervasive High Quality Access.
- Culture.

2.2.2 Cloud Computing Layers

- **Cloud Infrastructure**: the physical components to support cloud computing, including storage, processing resources, it allows the service provider to get details on which hardware specifications and applications work on it.

- **Cloud Storage – Storage as a service**: it is ability of renting storage for user, companies by uploading your data to their servers, formerly called Utility Computing

- **Cloud Platform – Platform as a service**: provide infrastructure, full platform for developing applications and web-based applications. Providing facilities for application design, application development, application testing, deployment, and hosting, as well as application services such as team collaboration, security, application versioning, and application instrumentation.

Developers can use their browsers (Client) or leverage the servers running in the cloud these servers may include web servers, application servers, and database engines.

Some service providers also offering application programming interfaces (APIs).

ProgrammableWeb.com list a lot of APIs on the internet, with Google Maps, Flickr, YouTube, and Amazon. Platforms are generally assumed to be part of complex architecture that will support different organization that use the same platform infrastructure.

Force.com began as a software application provider supporting SalesForce.com APIs and development tools and it becomes more general platform as a service provider for customer offering internet-based software.

- **Cloud Services – Components as a service:** this layer include definition of software components, run in a distributed environment, across the commercial internet.

- **Cloud Applications – Software as a service:** it one of the well-known type of cloud computing and there are many service provider of this type. It relies on moving the using of software from desktop to cloud for example instead on installing Adobe Photoshop on the desktop you can use version (called Express) on the cloud and upload your image and work on it. Also Google has Google Doc to edit document, presentation online, Google also has Google Calendar and there are many.

- **Cloud Clients:** focuses on the distribution of personal data and business across servers on the internet. People may upload their personal data to Facebook, Twitter, also upload images to Flickr, banking data in bank servers (Raines G., 2009).

Chapter Three

Software as a Service

3.1 Software as a service

The research will focus on the area of software engineering for SaaS software to control the nature of changed requirements for users and also to accommodate different needs for different users, different culture and different process flow to find adaptable, acceptable methodologies that can help the service provide to take this consideration and accommodate it if happened without affecting other user's workflow, culture setting, business process, and layout.

In software as a service (SaaS) the software deployed on the service provider and hosted in their datacenter, customers have access to the application across internet this will helps customer to eliminate the need to install, update, upgrade and run the application on their computers, all process of managing the software is handled by the service provider e.g. version control, hotfixes, updates, backup, security (Raines G., 2009).

Each time the user logs in to site (application) user gets the latest version of the software. The service (application) provider offering a very scalable web application using a multi-tiered web architecture, and implemented on a considerable infrastructure.

The disadvantage is that the customer will depend on software that completely dependence on the underlying network if the network down the application isn't available whereas the in the desktop application the application will not depend on the internet or even network.

In SaaS instead on installing the application on the local computer you will use your browser (universal client) to access the application so, SaaS is an application that is hosted on a remote server and access by client through internet communication (Anothony T. Velte, Toby J. Velte, Robert Elsenpeter, 2010). E.g searching social network, and watching videos, and playing games online (Armando Fox, David Patterson, 2012). This model has been around for a few years (Klein S., Roggero H., 2012).

SaaS is refers basically to software in cloud. Not all SaaS are cloud systems, but most of them are cloud systems (Reese G., 2009).

Fig 3.1 Software as a Service client communication (Anothony T. Velte, Toby J. Velte, Robert Elsenpeter, 2010)

Because of SaaS is web-based software that available entirely through the web browser. The user of SaaS software doesn't care about where the software is host, what type of technology, operating system, infrastructure and even which programming language are using; and of course you are not required to install any application on your own computer (Reese G., 2009).

Simply think about SaaS as any of the email services offered by Microsoft (Live, Hotmail), Google (Gmail) and Yahoo! (Yahoo Mail) all of these provider host the applications in their own storage, infrastructure, and software platform;

all we need to get access through browser by entering username and password even for free or with payment (Anothony T. Velte, Toby J. Velte, Robert Elsenpeter, 2010).

Revolution in this area happened in 2007 at Facebook - after it went online by three years –when Facebook platform was launched. Facebook allowed third party developers to develop application that interact with the core Facebook features – like, comments, tags, and shared – and it used by many of users (Armando Fox, David Patterson, 2012).

Fig 3.2 Email service as example

3.1.1 SaaS Categories (Anothony T. Velte, Toby J. Velte, Robert Elsenpeter, 2010)

- **Line of Business Service**: these types of solutions are offered to companies and enterprise by subscription fees. These software category include business processes, and workflow e.g. Supply Chain Management (SCM), Customer Relationship Management (CRM), Sales Software, and many others.

- **Customer-Oriented Services**: these type of software are offer free without subscription fess the cloud provider benefits from advertisement e.g email service provider by Google, Microsoft, Yahoo, ..., etc, and also social networks e.g. Facebook, Instagram, Twitter and others, watching videos, playing games, and so on.

3.1.2 Advantages (Anothony T. Velte, Toby J. Velte, Robert Elsenpeter, 2010)

a- Customer Advantages

- o In-house development takes more time to develop because of the long implementation life cycles and the failure rate of the enterprise software.
- o Software license cost is lower than installed software in the computer.
- o SaaS eliminate the cost of installing and maintaining hardware, pay labor costs, and maintain the applications itself.
- o SaaS can be used to avoid the custom development cycles to get applications to the organization quickly.
- o SaaS vendors typically have very meticulous security audits.
- o SaaS the customer can get the latest version of the application. This helps the organization to save the upgrades and updates cost to invest on their own business.
- o SaaS allows the organization to focus on their own business.

b- Vendor Advantages

- o Financial benefits.
- o Vendors benefit more as more subscribes come online. They have a huge investment on their infrastructure (hardware, technology staff, process development, and storage).

c- Software Considerations

In traditional software:

- o User purchases a software package and license by paying a one-time fee.
- o The software becomes a property of the user who bought it (not the source code).
- o Support and updates are provided by the vendor under the terms of license agreement.

In SaaS:

- o No licensing. You pay for application through the use of a subscription.
- o Pay only for what you use. If you stop using the application, you stop paying.
- o The software is not installed on the user's computer.

3.1.3 SaaS Limitations (Anothony T. Velte, Toby J. Velte, Robert Elsenpeter, 2010)

- Technical obstacles to SaaS have included an effective, multitenant architecture. This has been become less and less of a problem due to virtualization, but designing an application to efficiently deliver it to thousands of customers via the internet is hard work.
- Software companies need to become service companies, you need customer services. A business model that is built on selling licensed software doesn't easily transform easily into subscription model very cleanly.
- There are many applications that are not ideal for SaaS. e.g the data schemes and transaction are very complex, and the customer's

configuration requirement vary from customer to customer in Business Intelligence applications (BI) and it also requires intensive processing, so it is not attractive to the vender to provide a service that cost high hardware infrastructure.

- The SaaS providers become more sophisticated in the customization of their offerings.
- It is difficult to switch between vendors.
- The software becomes a service so you can't customize for your own level you are limited by the vendor customization specification e.g. think about customization for email service you can't perform your own customization by providing a new functionality of a customized functionality that is suitable for you.

3.1.4 SaaS Summary

Cloud computing provides the scalable and dependable hardware computation and storage for SaaS (Fox A., Patterson D., 2012). And the internet provide the communication for SaaS (Fox A., Patterson D., 2012).

Service Oriented Architecture (SOA) just means an approach to software development where all the subsystems only available as external services, which means others can recombine them in different ways (Fox A., Patterson D., 2012).

The universal client (web browser) makes the Software as a Service more attractive for both customers and provider it makes it easier for customer to use the service and for the vender makes it easier to deliver and improve the service.

The agile software development process is popular for Software as a Service application and also there are many frameworks to support it (Fox A., Patterson D., 2012).

3.2 Platform as a Service (PaaS)

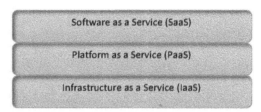

Fig 3-3: Three Major Layers for Cloud Computing

Considering PaaS as the ability to develop complete enterprise applications from the data to user interface with low cost and access a complete-class development environment (David S. Linthicum, 2009).

"PaaS provides a development platform with a set of services to assist application design, development, testing, deployment, monitoring, hosting on the cloud. It usually requires no software download or installation, and supports geographically distributed teams to work on projects collaboratively" (Tasi W., Sun X., Balasooriya J., 2010).

With PaaS no need to work with infrastructure level elements and low level network configuration, security, and load balancers; the vendor will configure all of these features for you, the vendor will provide full functioning operating system, secure environment, and configured platform to work on it. All you need is to focus on your development tasks and make it works as requested (Rizzo T., 2012).

For example the Microsoft Azure platform provides support for the latest version of the .NET framework. Azure's team responsible from configuring the platform, updating the operating system, updating the .NET framework, and any other configuration relating to the platform (Rizzo T., 2012).

"This type of service offering means you can focus on deploying your custom applications on the platform and can easily configure your applications to scale up or down as demands change" (Rizzo T., 2012)

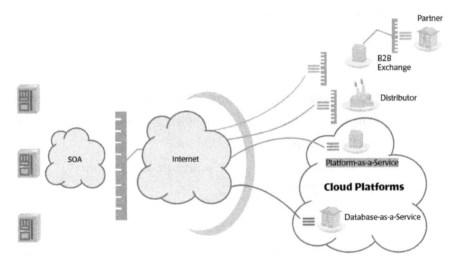

Fig 3-4: View of SOA and Cloud

Thinking of PaaS as one-stop shopping; all or required tasks can be done on the platform by building and deploying applications. The PaaS provides self-contained platforms with everything you need for application development and operational hosting (e.g Google App engine, Force.com) (David S. Linthicum, 2009).

3.2.1 PaaS Components (David S. Linthicum, 2009)

Design: ability to design your application and user interfaces.

Development: ability to design, develop, and test applications right out of the platform, on demand, using development tools that are delivered on demand.

Deployment: ability to test, and deliver the PaaS created applications. This means hosting the applications, typically accessing them visually, through a browser, or as web services.

Integration: ability to integrate the applications developed on your PaaS provider with SaaS applications or applications that may exist within your enterprise.

Storage: ability to provide persistence for the application, means an on-demand database or on-demand file storage.

Operations: ability to run the application over a long period of time, dealing with backup, restore, exception handling, and other things that add value to operations.

3.2.2 Example

"In order for Python code to be run, developers need the Python runtime and some sort of interface to expose the python code while it's running. Some PaaS providers support Python do it via a Web Server Gateway Interface (WSGI) interface. Apache, with the mode WSGI module, is one such way to run Python applications. Developers or PaaS providers need a WSGI script somewhere so the code can be loaded and exposed via a web address" (Michael P. McGrath, 2012).

"To visualize this, think about Apache and Python at a public web address with some storage on the back end and maybe a load balancer seems pretty simple to do. Don't forget though, that there's a whole set of dependencies in order to get to that point. Apache needs some sort of operating system to function. It needs to be configured, maintained and monitored. In cloud computing, this OS runs inside virtual machines" (Michael P. McGrath, 2012).

The disadvantage is that many of the platform-as-a-service vendors leverage proprietary programming languages and interfaces; thus, once your application is there, it may be difficult to move it to an on-premise server or another platform-as-a-service provider (David S. Linthicum, 2009).

"Many PaaS providers are providing multi-tenant solutions. This means that not only is the physical hardware shared among multiple virtual machines but the virtual machines themselves may have several different applications from server different customer on them" (Michael P. McGrath, 2012).

"PaaS today focuses almost entirely on web solutions. The components and end user interacts with are all web-based and because of this, most PaaS providers excel when it comes to large numbers of short lived process requests. PaaS providers have less polish when it comes to longer running, higher resource intensive jobs that cannot be broken down into smaller jobs. For example, a large batch processing job is likely best suited to be placed a level down at the IaaS layer because of the more fine controls over memory it provides. Scale out, not up, is becoming a common theme used throughout this matures, expect to see more offerings beyond web services" (Michael P. McGrath, 2012).

3.2.3 Impacts on IT professionals (Michael P. McGrath, 2012)

- **Developers**

  Focus on code and forget all about the underlying configuration and maintenance. By utilizing PaaS, developers simply need to pick the programming languages and features they want, match those requirements with a provider that has them, and start coding.

- **System Engineers/Administrators**

  Over the last decade, so much of what had become a sysadmin's job is technician work, like logging in, doing updates, and replacing hard drives; a lot of busy thankless works.

  Cloud computing provides a new way for admins and engineers to get back to focusing on the complicated interconnected systems that should be their jobs.

- **Architects/Management**

  Architects like the flexibility PaaS provides. Individual computing needs, like database, can be used without requiring internal expertise for running it. In a rapidly changing environment, this flexibility is extremely useful. Prototypes can be put together in days, not weeks or months. Technology can now be evaluated quickly and directly instead of having to rely on videos and sales pitch.

Management likes the cost structure. No longer do projects require a large initial capital investment. These research and development costs are very tiny operating expenditures if they cost anything at all.

3.2.4 Development Workflow (Michael P. McGrath, 2012)

The current development workflow in the cloud isn't that different from a traditional workflow except it happens more quickly, it might look like this:

1. Write code.
2. Test code.
3. Commit code.
4. Push code.
5. QA test.
6. Declare/Tag release.

There is a little requirement from the developer local compute power to develop a software (service) in cloud; tooling and testing stacks can be used with this workflow quickly and cheaply. Also it supports continuous integration, unit tests, builds and just anything imaginable in a development environment.

"PaaS makes it so easy to run code remotely that options are now available to do all development in the cloud. Entire IDE's exist using just a browser. All code, all everything is stored remotely" (Michael P. McGrath, 2012).

3.2.5 Automated Testing (Michael P. McGrath, 2012)

Testing is important to increase the reliability of software/code and find bugs early before they reach the end users (consumers). So the automated test is very important to ensure the reliability of the services.

No PaaS service will write unit tests for you but some offer ways to integrate testing as part of deployment process. For example Resd Hat's OpenShift and Cloudbees both offer continuous integration. Repositories can be setup to test code every commit. This happens server side so developers don't have to give up their workstation to run those test. Also, proper notifications and event handlers can be configured on success and failure scenarios to communicate with the entire team.

"In addition to unit testing, functional testing can be done in pre-production environments; PaaS makes it much easier to script the creation of dedicated environments for testing for testing. Functional tests can be done in an environment that is nearly identical to production. Once created, testing can be done to find performance and other issues. It's best practice to do these test regularly and PaaS makes it easier than ever to do them" (Michael P. McGrath, 2012).

3.2.6 PaaS Summary

PaaS providing platform for developing software as cloud based environment, developers do not need to install or configure any software in their own PCs all the need is to use browsers and write their code. The code will be interpreted and compiled in the cloud provider servers; there are many limitations for developing applications in cloud environment, cloud provider should limit code capabilities for some types of code to make sure they are secure from malicious programmers (users).

Chapter Four

Analysis of SDLC for Cloud Computing

4.1. Software Development Life Cycle

SDLC (Systems Development Life Cycle or Software Development Life Cycle) also referred to as the Application Development Life Cycle. SDLC is a framework that defines tasks to be performed and used by system engineers and system developers. It consists of many phases such as requirement gathering, designing, implementation, testing, and deployment.

To manage the complexity of computer systems a number of SDLC models or methodologies have been created, each one of these methodologies has it is own advantages and disadvantages and applicability in one or more than situation.

Some types of SDLC models or methodologies are waterfall, spiral, agile software development (XP, Scrum), and rapid prototyping, incremental and synchronize and stabilize.

As cloud computing is based on distributed network and virtualized environment allowing multi-tenancy, this nature make the traditional SDLC frameworks challenged and need to be more adaptable for this nature.

4.2 SDLC Phases (Mark S. Merkow, Raghavan L., 2010):

4.2.1 SDLC Phase Zero – Developer Training

Even though training does not fit directly into any particular SDLC phase, it plays a very important role in improving the overall quality of developed software.

Anyone that involved in the development of the software should meet the prerequisites of the software development environment. e.g they may undergo security training that explains the responsibilities of their role, also may undergo a cloud training to provide them with knowledge for developing a software applicable for cloud computing.

4.2.2 SDLC Phase One: Requirements gathering and analysis

"The hardest single part of building a software system is deciding what to build. No other part of the conceptual work is as difficult in establishing the detailed technical requirements, including the interfaces to people, to machines, and to other software systems. No other part of the work so cripples the results if done wrong. No other part is more difficult to rectify later. Therefore, the most important function that the software builder performs for the client is the iterative extraction and refinement of the product requirements." (Brooks, F.P, 1995)

The documentation to describe the behavior required from the software before the software designed, build and tested are called software requirements (Andrew Stellman, Jennifer Greene, 2005).

Requirements analysts (or business analysts) build software requirements specifications through requirements elicitation (Andrew Stellman, Jennifer Greene, 2005)

- Interviews with the users, stakeholders and anyone else whose perspective needs to be taken into account during the design, development and testing of the software.

32

- Observation of the users at work.
- Distribution of discussion summaries to verify the data gathered in interviews.

There are two types of requirements (Stellman A., Greene J., 2005):

- **Functional requirements**: define the outward behavior of the software project.
  The list of features the user will see and be able to use when they fire up the system (Dooley J., 2011).

- **Non-Functional requirements**: define characteristics of the software which do not change its behavior.

4.2.3 SDLC Phase Two: Systems Design:

"Design is messy. Even if you completely understand the problem requirements (it's a tame problem), you typically have many alternatives to consider when you're designing a software solution" (Dooley J., 2011).

To show how requirements will be implemented technically design will handle this task (Stellman A., Greene J., 2005).

4.2.3.1 Desirable Design Characteristics (Dooley J., 2011):

- **Fitness of purpose**: the design must work, and work correctly in the sense that it must satisfy the requirements.

- **Separation of concerns**: separate out functional pieces of the design cleanly in order to facilitate ease of maintenance and simplicity.

- **Simplicity**: the design should be as simple as possible. This will let others understand what you're up to.

- **Ease of maintenance**: a simple, understandable design is amenable to change.

- **Loose coupling**: when you are separating your design into either modules or in object0oriented design, into classes, the degree to which the classes depend on each other is called coupling. Tightly coupled modules may share data or procedures. This means that a change in one module is much more likely to lead to requirement change into the other module. Loosely coupled modules, on the other hand, are connected solely by their interfaces. Any data they both need must be passed between procedures or methods via an interface. Loosely coupled modules hide the details of how they perform operations from other modules, sharing only their interfaces.

- **High cohesion**: the complement of loose coupling is high cohesion. Cohesion within a module is the degree to which the module is self-contained with regards both to the data it holds and the operations that act on the data.

- **Extensibility**: an outgrowth of simplicity and coupling is the ability to add new features to the design easily.

- **Portability**: keeping in mind that the software may need to be ported to another platform.

4.2.4 SDLC Phase Three: Development

The goal of this phase is to actually write the code, consume exiting services and APIs, it is one of the most important phases in which you have to make sure this code is written with best practices, and self-documented.

4.2.5 SDLC Phase Four: Testing Phase

The goal of software testing is to make sure that the product does what the users and stakeholders need it to do (Stellman A., Greene J., 2005).

Software testers review the final product to make sure that the initial requirements have been met (Stellman A., Greene J., 2005).

4.2.6 SDLC Phase Five: Deployment Phase

In this phase you deploy the application so it can be used by the end users, and it is configured to achieve their purpose of the software.

4.3 Important Note for Cloud provider

To become cloud provider it is important to understand that

- The cloud computing area is driven by the business and not by technical organizations. It is not a fight between features and functions; it is a battle between services best supporting customer's business.
- Security is critical. Using services means to trust the cloud provider. This trust must be on a secure infrastructure and as well in processes and support.
- Cloud computing dose not equal traditional outsourcing. Having the right skillset is vital.

- Clearly defining the services upfront is key for cloud providers. Potential customers have industry vertical specific requirement and are constrained by various legal regulations, which may include enforcement for data being stored and processed within close legal proximity to their jurisdiction such as within national boundaries. Cloud providers need to understand and fulfill these to be successful.

4.4 Impact of Cloud Computing in SDLC

The important questions are will traditional SDLC frameworks be suitable completely for the cloud SDLC? And how is traditional SDLC different from Cloud SDLC?

To answer the first question investigation of the impact cloud computing in the traditional SDLC will be conducted in the following paragraphs.

A paradigm shift occurs in a number of areas such as software development, IT usage, and software service industries, this shift caused by the cloud computing and the natural extension to the Service oriented Architecture (SOA) and the World Wide Web (WWW) (Mahmood Z., Saeed S., 2013).

The impact on the software development life cycle needs special attentions. Some key aspects will be used to investigate this impact:

- Privacy Requirements.
- Design Methodologies.
- Testing Methodologies.

- Configuration Management.

"To truly benefit from cloud environment, software development teams should look at the cloud computing environment as a new development paradigm and leverage it to lead to differentiated value" (Mahmood Z., Saeed S., 2013).

4.4.1 Requirement Analysis:

In general the thought of industry about cloud as an enabler or rather a solution makes the industry believes that there is no bearing on the requirements.

To successfully moving to cloud a guidelines and checklist that aid in requirement analysis are required. The requirements may be functional or non-functional most of the requirements that need an assessment in cloud are non-functional requirements in nature. **These include**:

- **Cloud assessment**:
  To evaluate the cloud readiness and applicability for an enterprise. This assessment determines the return on the investment for the enterprise. The enterprise may create tools to aid the projects to perform assessment.

- **Cloud usage pattern identification and capturing data points to support requirement analysis based on usage patterns**.
  - o Constant usage of cloud resources over time.
    For example the availability of the applications, application downtime and uptime, data loss limits in case of application crash.
  - o Cyclic Internal Load.

For example batch jobs that applied to the business and scheduled to execute at specific time, I/O volume required to satisfy business process.

o Cyclic External Load.

"Includes applications that are developed to serve a particular demand, like publishing examination results/election campaign and sites related to entertainment" (Mahmood Z., Saeed S., 2013).

o Spiked Internal Load.

For example, number of users accessing the system, network bandwidth and expected delay, variety of data that is used in day-to-day business, processes that can execute site by site.

o Spiked External Load.

Applies to applications that should be able to handle sudden load which come from an external source e.g. customers, vendors, and public users.

For example limit to access the application, country-level regulations to handle the load, industry-level regulations to handle the load.

o Steady Growth over time.

Cost of maintaining application on cloud; as users are added as more resources are required.

4.4.2 Architecture

On-promise hosted/deployed applications architecture is different than cloud environment architecture. The distributed nature of cloud computing led to emergence of verities of design and architecture principles. Cloud computing should operate on a network which is capable of handling massive data transactions so there will be high I/O volume/velocity.

Software quality is demanded increasingly from clients, so the enterprise should produces software that can be adaptable to the new environments without degrading on the existing parameter of quality.

4.4.3 Design

"The design patterns guide the composition of modules into complete systems. In addition to existing design patterns and number of other common patterns, applications developed for distributed environments need to work in B2C services and use respective credentials while accessing. Application designers should start thinking of designing applications for failure analysis and parallelism to avail the cloud infrastructure" (Mahmood Z., Saeed S., 2013).

4.4.3.1 Design for Parallelism

Designing and programming to leverage multiple cores and multiple processors is called parallel programming. CPU core has get a significant increase in the number of cores and the speed of the CPU the CPU manufacturers are working on this area hardly. The number of extra cores makes the standard threading concept will not automatically run faster as expected.

All applications in the server-based architecture in distributed environment should leverage the multiple cores, where each thread can independently handle a separate request.

To leverage parallelism in distributed environment, the design should

- Partition computationally intensive code into multiple chunks.

- Execute those chunks in parallel implementing multithreading and asynchronous communications between these independent threads.
- Collate the results once execution is completed in a thread-safe mode.

Parallelism can be applied at

- Data Level

  Data is partitioned across thread so that when multiple tasks need to perform on many data values, threads can perform similar set of tasks on a subset of data.

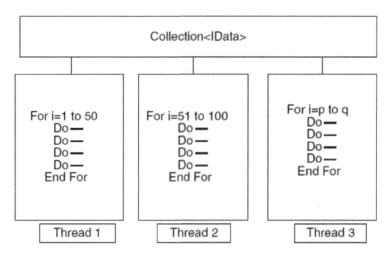

Fig 4-1: tasks and threads

- Task Level

  The tasks execute simultaneously on multiple cores processing many different functions across data. As part of workflow defined for the context communication between threads takes place.

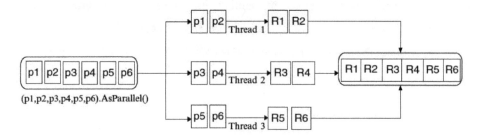

Fig 4-2: Task level and threads

4.4.4 Build

The additional impacts during build phase are typically centered on the organizations' effort to reduce cost. The impacts are more in terms of planning and prioritization rather than software build. The key questions are:

- How often the continuous integration should deploy on cloud?
- Provisioning of development and testing environment, which the organization decides the host as a cloud service.

4.4.5 Testing

Recent years software testing got a significant automation.

Due to the diversity and availability of resources in cloud environment the testing of applications that deployed into cloud will be a little cumbersome.

Homogeneity and heterogeneity of network, and services and the environment in which the application is distributed also the unpredictable latency in network make the testing more complex and need a special consideration.

"The design of a system should emphasize decoupling, and each decoupled component should be implemented to allow independent testing. Modularization of a system will reduce testing effort. Implementing test automation process will be a little tricky in cloud environment" (Mahmood Z., Saeed S., 2013).

4.4.6 Version Control and Configuration Management

There is a lack of existing configuration management and version control tools especially in different kinds of artifacts and monitoring different environments for different kind of deployments like partial deployment, patch releases, and full and complete deployment, and creating respective rollback scenarios is very difficult to achieve using the currently available tools.

The changes in software in the cloud computing environment are distributed because of the distributed nature of cloud computing environment the configuration management systems should ensure the changes happening across environments and provide a consolidated view of application stack.

Monitoring and controlling of configuration changes should be managed across various layers and environments of applications software includes Web application servers, databases, different third-party components, sharewares, operating systems, and hardware.

To implement a successful cloud computing software the team should take all of the consideration on their mind information gathering, design, development, testing, version control and configuration management, cultural, availability, security, multi-tenancy and all non-functional requirement into considerations and also the agility of the software.

The development platform environment in the cloud computing encourages use of agile methodologies.

In today's fast changing technological world, the need for faster development processes, higher developer productivity and adaptation to certain technological trends, makes it even more important for the development teams to have the flexibility and robustness of cloud as well as maturity in SDLC framework which can be accommodated in the cloud computing environments.

SDLC for Cloud Computing will be different than traditional SDLC in following ways

- Inclination towards Agile Methodologies:

  Cloud SDLC can utilize methodologies such as Agile SDLC (using SCRUM or IBM Rational Unified Process). These are designed for iterative approach to development and fast deployment lifecycles.

- Customizable SDLC framework for different stages:
  Cloud computing SDLC must have the capabilities to be customized according to the requirements of the project due to change in the effort levels and implementation speeds. In other words the elasticity and robustness of cloud computing environment (to be able to scale-up and scale-down on-demand) can best be utilized if the SDLCs for cloud are customizable in the integrated IDEs and ALMs in the cloud.

- Installation and configuration guidelines:

SDLC for cloud must provide implementation approach and guidelines for installation for installation and configuration of the cloud environment that is being erected, depending upon its size. The guidelines must ensure that installation and configuration of infrastructure and application environment is completed appropriately for different stages of SDLC including operations and maintenance, these guidelines are the key to differentiating SDLC for cloud from traditional SDLC. This is so because the infrastructure set-up for computing environments and other application environments in the cloud are very different from the traditional on-promise IT stacks, as cloud is based on distributed network and virtualized environment allowing multi-tenancy.

Chapter Five

Recommended SDLC characteristics

5.1. Software Agility

5.1.1 Agile software development

Nowadays the nature of software is more agile by changing in many elements that affect software development like politics, organization, regulations, marketing strategies and many others. To provide a successful software as a service (SaaS) software for cloud paradigm the software should be agile and very flexible to adapt changes in any element that affect software development.

We can utilize methodologies such as Agile SDLC (using SCRUM, XP, or IBM Rational Unified Process). These methodologies can be designed for iterative approach to development and fast deployment lifecycles (Mahmood Z., Saeed S., 2013).

"Cloud computing SDLC must have the capabilities to be customized according to the requirements of the project due to change in the effort levels and implementation speeds. In other words the elasticity and robustness of cloud computing environment (**to be able to scale-up and scale-down on-demand**) can best be utilized if the SDLCs for cloud are customizable in the integrated IDEs and ALMs in the cloud" (Mahmood Z., Saeed S., 2013).

5.1.2. Agile Methodologies and PaaS

For software development and project management agile methodologies take the interactive and iterative approach to gather requirements from the customer for software development and project management (Mahmood Z., Saeed S., 2013).

"Its aim is to provide flexibility to the developers, managers and the end user in order to arrive at the optimal (software) solution for customer" (Mahmood Z., Saeed S., 2013).

"In an era where time-to-market and adding value to the business to outsmart the competition have taken the center stage, agile development methodologies and PaaS make a priceless combination" (Mahmood Z., Saeed S., 2013).

5.1.3. 'PaaS' value added to the Agile

PaaS (Platform as a Service) is a utility service for developing software applications where developers do not have to b other about installing the OS, storage capacities or hosting capabilities (Mahmood Z., Saeed S., 2013).

PaaS users have to bother only about the pay per use cost with many of cloud computing providers, also there is a free PaaS platforms. The PaaS service provider provides the entire setup required to develop a software application – the OS, the upgrades, the hosting capabilities and the network and data security (Mahmood Z., Saeed S., 2013).

"With PaaS, developers and project managers can take the iterative approach where the requirements can be gathered based on stages of development. The solutions can be delivered as a prototype with the available set of data and then the iterations can be taken from there to arrive at the best solution" (Mahmood Z., Saeed S., 2013).

"PaaS reinforces the agile development and management methodologies, which the organizations strive to, in order to improve the customer responsiveness and reduce the time-to-deliver the solutions to the stakeholders. In other words, it is best to call PaaS as 'agile ready' framework and the new age method to go for development activities" (Mahmood Z., Saeed S., 2013).

Where the uncertainty prevails high and the customer is not sure of his needs or the project is too large to be documented in totality at on go Agile with PaaS is very ideal to those cases (Mahmood Z., Saeed S., 2013). "In such a situation, if the service providers make use of PaaS, then they can customize and incorporate change is the coding faster as they do not have to start from scratch" (Mahmood Z., Saeed S., 2013).

5.1.4. Agile Project Management

"Agile project management is a practice for managing development projects in a highly interactive and flexible way. It takes the iterative approach to determine the requirements of the customers" (Mahmood Z., Saeed S., 2013).

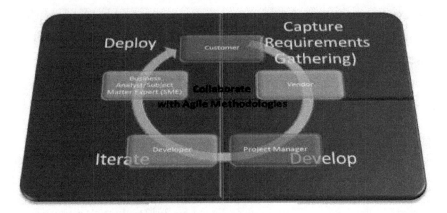

Fig 5.1 Pass Framework

5.2. Cloud to the Developer

When you developing for the cloud, you can break things down to building blocks, buy pieces from service providers, and put them together instead of buying a computer and running software on it (Mark C. Chu-Carroll, 2011).

For developers, a bigger change introduces in cloud computing in the concept of building applications, you need to think about you're not building a piece of software to sell to your customers (e.g. to-do list application) you're building a service for the customers to consume (e.g. to-do list service). The understanding of the difference is important: "you need to design application around the idea that it's a service you're going to install on their computers. Your customers are going to choose a service based on the tasks they want to accomplish, so your application needs to be designed with the task in mind, and you must provide it in the most flexible way possible" (Mark C. Chu-Carroll, 2011).

For example, if you want to build a to-do list application for a desktop computer, it's fairly straightforward process. There are lots of variations in how you can arrange the UI – after all, why would you need more than one? And you'd build it mainly for single user. If you are developing this to-do list application for the cloud, thought you'd want multiple UIs: at the very least, you'd want one UI for people accessing your service using their desktop computer and one for people using a mobile browser on a cell phone. You'd probably want to provide an open interface that other people cloud uses for building clients for other devices. And you'd need to design it for multiple users; if you can put application in the cloud, there's only one program, but it can be used by lots of people. So you need to design it around the assumption that even if users never work together using your application, it's still a multi-user system (Mark C. Chu-Carroll, 2011).

The most exciting aspect of cloud computing for developers is its scalability. When you're developing a program in the cloud, you can write a simple code to be used by one or more users, and then, without changing any line of code, that program can scale up to support millions of users. As you get more users all you need is to buy more resources and the program will just work (Mark C. Chu-Carroll, 2011).

5.3. Web Based Applications

Web applications are design to be accessed from web browser. It is a combination of a server side scripts (e.g. ASP, PHP, … etc.) and client side script (HTML, JavaScript, … etc.) these tools are commonly used to develop web applications.

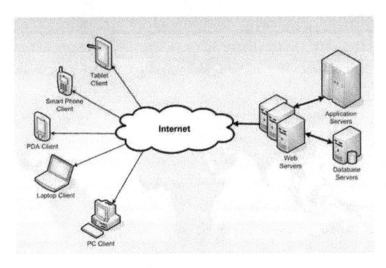

Fig 5-2: Web based applications structure

"Cloud services, in the form of centralized web-based applications, also appeal to the IT professional. One instance of an application hosted in the cloud is cheaper and easier to manage than individual copies of similar software installed on each user's desktop PC" (Miller M., 2008).

A web Service is an application that operates over a network – typically, over the internet. A web service is an API that can be accessed over the internet. The service is invoked by client and then executed on a remote system that hosts the requested services (Miller M., 2008).

Rather than developing all of the functionality by yourself web services API helps developers to shared functionality from another service provider e.g. you can use Google API if your application implements functionality of maps and other services that Google API provides. Also you can implement

51

authentication through Microsoft active directory by use their services (Miller M., 2008).

Web services have many advantages that include faster and lower cost of developing applications (Miller M., 2008).

"In essence, web services keep developers from having to reinvent the wheel every time they develop a new application. By reusing code from the web services provider, they get a jump-start on the development of their own applications" (Miller M., 2008).

5.4 Cloud provider Involvement

In any phase of cloud computing software development cloud server provider should be involved.

5.5. Service-Oriented Architecture (SOA) (SATRUN 2011):

A way of designing, developing, deploying, and managing systems characterized by coarse-grained services that represent reusable functionality.

Service consumers compose applications or systems using functionality provided by these services through standard interfaces.

The services in a cloud can be defined as services in a SOA context.

As an example, some of the cloud environments presented earlier offer web services interfaces to their services (one specific implementation of SOA).

A cloud infrastructure could be built on top on an SOA infrastructure by adding a layer or virtualization and self-provisioning.

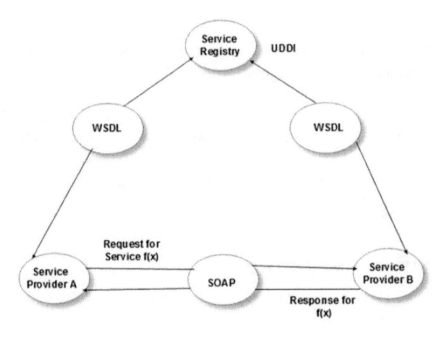

Fig 5-3: SOA Architecture

Chapter Six

Conclusion and Recommendation

6.1 Conclusion

This research is aimed to investigate cloud computing paradigm, software development life cycle to provide a characteristics for cloud computing software development life cycle. The purpose is to provide a characteristic to develop software for cloud paradigm or Software as a Service (SaaS).

The proposed characteristics of the methodology include web service development, SOA Software Oriented Architecture, Agile software engineering methodologies that involve cloud provider to help on developing software by using existing API from other software developer of current cloud computing developer.

6.2 Recommendation

1. Understanding existing API available to use by cloud can be helpful to reduce development time e.g. like Google API, Amazon web services, etc...
2. Involving cloud computing provider from early state in developing software, involving should be at least from the beginning of analysis phase.
3. When developing any service/utility reusability should be considered.
4. Developer should be aware about cloud computing paradigm and training in this area should be done and maintained.

6.3 Future Work

Researchers can take this research as a beginning step on cloud computing and software engineering methodologies because cloud computing is hot topic. The research provides highlights on developing for cloud but it doesn't provide a step by step approach by exploring SCRUM, or XP agile methodologies.

Researchers can explore more options and provide change on agile methodologies best practice and techniques.

6.4 Limitation

This research won't provide a step by step guide for developing in cloud it provide characteristics of SDLC (software development life cycle) for cloud computing. These characteristics should be considered when thinking or developing for cloud.

References

1. Andrew Stellman, Jennifer Greene, Applied Software Project Management 1st edition, O'Reilly, Nov. 2005.

2. Anthony T. Velte, Toby J. Velte, and Robert Elsenpeter. Cloud Computing A Practical Approach. Mc Graw Hill, 2010.

3. Architecting for Change, Sixth Annual SEI Architecture Technology User Network Conference, SATURN 2010.

4. Armando Fox and David Patterson, Engineering Long-Lasting Software: Agile Approach Using SaaS and Cloud Computing, Beta Edition 0.9.0 Aug. 2012.

5. Brooks, F.P. The Mythical Man-Month: Essays on Software Engineering, Silver Anniversary Edition. (Boston, MA: Addison-Wesley, 1995).

6. David S. Linticum, Cloud Computing and SOA Convergence in Your Enterprise A Step-by-Step Guide, Addison-Wesley Information Technology Series, Pearosn Education, Inc, 2009,

7. Eric A. Marks, and Bob Lozano, Executive's Guide to Cloud Computing, WILEY, John Wiley & Sons, Inc., 2010.

8. Gautam Shroff, Enterprise Cloud Computing Technology, Architecture, Applications. Cambridge University Press, 2010.

9. Geoffrey Raines, Cloud Computing and SOA. Service-Oriented Architecture (SOA) Series, Systems Engineering at MITRE, MITRE, 2009.

10. George Reese, Cloud Application Architectures, Building Applications and Infrastructure in the Cloud, O'Reilly, April 2009.

11. I. Foster, Y.Zhau, R. Loan, and S. Lu. "Cloud Computing and Grid Computing: 360-Degree Compared." Grid Computing Environments Workshop, 2008.

12. John Dooley, Software Development and Professional Practice, Apress, 2011.

13. Mark C. Chu-Carroll, Code in the Cloud Programming Google AppEngine, The Pragmatic Bookshelf, April 2011.

14. Mark C. Chu-Carroll, Code in the Cloud Programming Google AppEngine, The Pragmatic Bookshelf, April 2011.

15. Mark S. Merkow, Lakshmikanth Raghavan, Secure and Resilient Software Development, Auerbach Publications, June 2010.

16. Michael Miller, Cloud Computing: Web-Based Applications That Change the Way You Work and Collaborate Online, Que, 2008

17. Michael P. McGrath, Unleash the Power of Cloud Computing - Understanding PaaS, O'Reilly, 2012.

18. Scott Klein and Herve Roggero, Pro SQL Database for Windows Azure SQL Server in the Cloud 2nd edition, Apress, 2012.

19. Scott Klein and Herve Roggero, Pro SQL Database for Windows Azure, SQL Server in the cloud, Apress, 2012.

20. Tom Rizzo, Programming Microsoft's Clouds Azure and Office 365, Jhon Wiley & Sons, Inc., 2012.

21. Wei-Tek Tsai, Xin Sun, Janaka Balasooriya, Service-Oriented Cloud Computing Architecture, Seventh International Conference on Information Technology, 2010.

22. Zaigham Mahmood, Saqib Saeed, Software Engineering Frameworks for the Cloud Computing Paradigm, Springer, 2013.

www.ingramcontent.com/pod-product-compliance
Lightning Source LLC
LaVergne TN
LVHW042347060326
832902LV00006B/447